flower crowns & fearsome things

amanda lovelace

flower
crowns
&
fearsome
things

amanda lovelace

Andrews McMeel
PUBLISHING®

books by amanda lovelace

the

WoMEN are some KiND of MAGiC

series:

the princess saves herself in this one (#1)
the witch doesn't burn in this one (#2)
the mermaid's voice returns in this one (#3)

slay those dragons: a journal for writing your own story

believe in your own magic: a 45-card oracle deck & guidebook

***

the
things that h(a)unt
duology:

to make monsters out of girls (#1)
to drink coffee with a ghost (#2)

***

the
you are your own fairy tale
series:

break your glass slippers (#1)
shine your icy crown (#2)

for those who
wish to raise hell most elegantly.

trigger warning

this book contains
sensitive material relating to:

intimate partner abuse,
sexual assault,
cheating,
child abuse,
trauma,
death,
violence,
misogyny,
body image,
eating disorders,
alcohol,
fire,

& possibly more.

remember to practice self-care
before, during, & after
reading.

a note from the author

merry meet!

there is a beloved goddess from greek mythology you may or may not be familiar with. her name is persephone. she's fascinating for an endless list of reasons, including the fact that she's considered to be both the goddess of spring as well as the queen of the underworld, making her quite the complicated woman, in my humble opinion.

in this collection, i explore how, in this modern age, we, too, are often equal parts soft & fierce.

remember: there is no need to choose one or the other.

laced with love,
amanda

who said you can't
wear a flower crown
& still remain
a fearsome thing?

—*make persephone proud.*

she cries just as much when
she's completely happy
as she does when
she's utterly devastated.

(she likes to think it's enough to
water wildflower meadows.)

they may call her *pathetic*.
they may call her *dramatic*.
they may call her a *baby*.

but she thinks it's a blessing
to feel everything so much.

—*goddess of spring.*

she has always sparked
more fear than lust in the hearts of men.

she doesn't need their chocolate.
she doesn't need their diamonds.
she doesn't need their money.

all of those things
she can give to herself.

when he sent her roses,
she burned them all
& then planted her own,
& they were all the more lovely for it.

—*queen of the underworld.*

never once has she felt as if
she's interesting enough to be
the daring heroine of her own story,
& she's oddly okay with that.

—she likes being nobody.

she is not strong
because
she wields a sword.

she's strong
&
she wields a sword.

get it right.

—she never needed a weapon to be powerful.

to everyone who has a bad day
& tries to take it out on me:

i send you love & light.

i pray your bitterness
is replaced with sweetness.

i pray that your next day
is a much kinder one.

i pray you go easier on yourself
& those around you.

—*because that's what everyone deserves.*

everyone loves a strong woman
until that woman
no longer tolerates their bullshit.

—*the age-old proverb.*

i forgive everyone who has ever hurt me,
whether by chance or on purpose.

they all ask me, in awe,
"how do you do it?"

& here's what i say:

"what's more painful—
holding petals or holding prickles?"

—*rose.*

contrary to popular belief,
i have no interest in vengeance.

the thing about karma
is that she's a bitch
& she's a bitch that can always
be counted on,

so i leave everything in her
all-too-eager hands.

—*the threefold law.*

every time she thinks
she's finally found the real thing—

her epic, once-in-a-lifetime love—

they make it clear that
they only ever wanted one thing—

a stroke to their ego.

—will i ever be enough for someone?

treat her with decency—

even when she doesn't
share your blood.

even when she
calls you out.

even when you don't see her
as *one of the guys.*

even when she
turns down your advances.

even when you aren't
attracted to her.

—could the bar get any lower?

if every other girl is queen anne's lace,
then i'm poison hemlock.

at first glance,
we look exactly the same,

until someone gets too close
& they realize i'm not worth the trouble.

—*sigh.*

being friends with girls isn't
too much drama,

but you know what *is?*

constantly trying to
burn your sisters
at the fucking stake
out of pettiness
& resentment

when you could
just support them instead.

—*commit to putting out more fires than you start.*

she always says *sorry* or *excuse me*
before inserting herself
into a conversation,

& she wonders who
taught her to do that

because she's begun to notice
that he never so much as thinks twice
before speaking his mind.

—what's it like to be so bold?

i refuse to be ashamed
of taking up my rightful space.

i refuse to apologize
for daring to have an opinion.

—*it's a pleasure to disappoint you.*

when someone she loves is sad,
she stops at nothing to
make sure they feel better.

if she could, she would magic
a double rainbow into the sky
just to see a small smile on their face,

even though she can't think of
a single soul in her life
who would do the same for her.

—being the dependable friend is difficult sometimes.

she's not waiting for you to
c a l l
her back.

she's not waiting for you to
t e x t
her back.

she's not waiting for you to
h a v e
her back.

—she's doing fine on her own.

from the tallest tree
a sparrow dropped,
his neck cracking
on the solid earth.

the girl cupped him
with soft hands
& began to weep,
saying to no one,

"how tragic it is
for someone to die
when they had so many
more places to fly."

—*will i get to do all of the things i want to do?*

when she thinks of her demise, she smiles,
for she knows that she's
only going to grow more formidable
with each life she lives.

—*just you wait & see.*

one day, years from now,
when the world stops ending,
the first thing i will do
is come within six feet of you.

i will hold your face.
i will no longer be afraid.

—*we're going to make it, you & i.*

when i wear a mask,
not only am i protecting
the lives of myself & others,

but

nobody tells me to smile,
to look less intimidating
or prettier for them.

better yet,

nobody can see me mouthing
go   to   hell
with my perfect lipstick mouth.

—at last.

they know her as *the girl who sees signs in everything.* at her core, she knows that the dragonflies are probably just dragonflies & the songbirds are probably just songbirds—not guardian angels in disguise, not departed loved ones delivering messages of comfort & reassurance. but if you think that will ever stop her, then you'd be horribly mistaken, for experience has taught her that the faith in miracles is more important than the presence of them. after all, that's often what creates them in the first place.

—hope is essential.

if someone had to describe her, they would probably say that she's *the girl who doesn't believe in anything.* in other words, she doesn't believe that her life is inevitable. she doesn't believe that tarot cards have the ability to predict her future, as though it's already been written in the stars; rather, she believes they reveal mere possibilities, & every choice she makes from there weaves her fate. but in that way, i guess you could say she does believe in one thing.

—*herself.*

she would love nothing more than to
leave a heart-shaped tattoo on
a world filled with so much hatred—

to honor each & every woman
who came before her.

—she can't help feeling like she's letting them down.

would it be nice if my loved ones
were proud of me?

of course,

but i can't depend on
the approval of others alone.

it's never guaranteed.

what matters more to me is
finding pride in myself.

—i'm the only one who will be in my life forever.

is it normal for a father
to make you feel like
your voice is so small
it doesn't even matter?

—*just a stupid, silly girl.*

save everyone some trouble
& learn to respect women
before you have a daughter.

i hate to break it to you,
but you are not the god of her.

she is not yours to cage.
she is not yours to control.

she is not livestock
that belongs to you alone,
nor does she have to
obey your every command.

—*treat her with the same reverence as a goddess.*

when she's finally alone
& dares to explore herself,

she's filled with nothing
but immense guilt & shame,

for she has always been told that
her body is not her own—

that it should be saved for her
future husband to worship.

—*teach her that there's nothing wrong with
worshipping herself first.*

if you're so offended by the idea
of me enjoying sex,

i suggest you do your best
to get over it.

remember:
if it's my body, then it's my choice.

& don't forget:
if it's my bed, then it's my business.

—it's not up for debate.

under the light of the full moon
she dances about wildly,
hoping an otherworldly being
will come whisk her away
& take her on a grand adventure.

—she's so done with reality.

why is it that we're always
the damsels in distress?

write more difficult women.
write more angry women.
write more unlikeable women.
write more cunning women.

write more women who revel
in their wickedness.

—*show our complexity.*

for once, i want to be someone
who is not too difficult to be loved back.

—*is that too much to ask?*

never again will i be the one
who gets down on her
two bruised knees like
she's getting ready to pray
only to beg him to stay.

—if you don't want me, it's your loss.

the boy is tall & pretty & sad.

—needless to say,
he stole her heart right out of her chest.

i think i finally understand why
men love dogs so much—

they're unquestionably loyal.
they're easy to command.

they hate me because i refuse to be
either of those things.

—*never will i roll over for anyone.*

tell me who your dream girl is.
give me a list a forest long.

i'll be her.

i'll be anyone you want me to be.

—i don't mind.

i am the water.
i am the wine.

i am the very magic that
turns one into the other.

meanwhile, he isn't shit.

why would i bother with someone
who simply cannot compare?

—it's called having standards.

it would be a lie if i said
i didn't wear this skirt
with the hope that you would
put your hand on my leg
while you drive.

—*you are my favorite possibility.*

this lipstick?
i wear it for me.

these lashes?
i wear them for me.

this eye shadow?
i wear it for me.

these heels?
i wear them for me.

this skintight outfit?
i wear it for me.

—*you're never even considered.*

he's all cloaks & daggers.
he's all smoke & mirrors.

like a novel with chapters
that always end on a cliff-hanger,

i never know what he's going to do next
& i'm nothing short of obsessed.

—*i can't stop turning his pages.*

she's equal parts glitter & hellfire.

once unleashed,
you won't be able to contain her.

—*he's never wanted someone so much.*

he's so misunderstood
& she's so committed
to being the first one to
understand him.

—*leather jackets & late-night conversations.*

don't you think it's funny how *bad boys*
are always deemed swoon-worthy,

while *bad girls* are usually perceived
as a threat to society?

—don't tell me sexism isn't real.

will you still think i'm lovely
if there's no gap between my thighs?

—*something every girl has had to wonder.*

i refuse to starve myself
to meet your ridiculous
qualifications for beauty.

i deal with enough
just for daring to exist.

i deserve warmth.
i deserve happiness.

i deserve freedom.

i deserve to wear a bathing suit
without worrying about
who may be offended by my rolls.

—*it's not worth my energy anymore.*

you don't have to do very much
to make her happy.

just let her wear your t-shirt
& read her fairy tales
until she falls asleep.

—*the only thing she needs is you.*

horror movies are her favorite,

but it's *not* because she wants someone
to come put their arm around her
& protect her during the scary parts.

it's because she likes being frightened
by something so much less dangerous
than walking alone to her car at night.

—*a movie could never murder her.*

covering you with
a blanket when you're cold—

lightly running fingertips
over your scalp—

bringing you your
favorite pancakes in bed—

folding your clothes
without being asked to—

surprising you with
perfectly made coffee.

—how she shows her love without words.

she agreed to be your girlfriend.
she did *not* agree to be your mother.

—she isn't responsible for you.

take me to the library.

let's find a dark corner
in front of the stacks
where they keep myths
about lovers who could
never measure up to us.

bite my neck.
show everyone i'm yours.

—*marked.*

don't make the mistake
of thinking you are the king of me.

you will never own me.

if we're to rule this castle together,
then you will be beside me,

—never in front of me.

sometimes she feels like
he wants to be the only
important person in her life.

his boyish charm transforms
into silent anger whenever
she gives her time to
someone other than him, so

when someone calls,
she presses *ignore*
as many times as it takes,

& when someone knocks,
she hides in the dark
until they finally leave.

—*it's a lonely life, but she doesn't want to fight anymore.*

if they have an unhealthy
fixation on honesty & loyalty,
then they're probably
hiding something from you
& they just want to make sure
that you're not committing
the same crimes they are.

—*that's what we refer to as a guilty conscience.*

i see your wandering eye.
i see your hypocrisy.

i see the way you look
away from me to look at her
like she's an otherworldly
phenomenon—

a nymph you can't resist.

it makes me want to wither
where i stand,

& my mother taught me
to be an *annual*,
never a *perennial.*

—once i leave, i won't be coming back.

i'm deleting you from my life
the same way you deleted
(almost) all of her texts.

—*the difference is i won't be as sloppy about it.*

i have a history of staying in places
i've long outgrown.

you see, i was always told to stay
as small as possible—

even if it's uncomfortable,
even if it hurts.

from this day forward,
i vow to let myself bloom freely—

even if others see me as an annoyance,
even if they see me as a weed.

—*wild violet.*

here's what i'm manifesting:

eventually, when he feels
the urge to check up on me
to make sure i'm still grieving
the oh-so-tragic loss of him,

he will find only celebration
for the life i took back.

—*happiness is the revenge, after all.*

when he placed his seeds on her tongue,
she felt like she had to say "yes"
because she was terrified of
what would happen if she said "no."

—*pomegranate.*

"but she was wearing a short skirt."
it doesn't matter.

"but she never screamed for help."
it doesn't matter.

"but she had a lot to drink."
it doesn't matter.

"but she waited so long to tell."
it doesn't matter.

"but she consented to it before."
it doesn't matter.

"but they were hopelessly in love."
it doesn't matter.

—believe her, no matter what.

as she layers concealer
over her bruises,
he almost looks sorry.

(mostly for himself.)

he tells her that the reason
he hurts her is *because*
he loves her so much.

—*in that moment, she knew she had to risk it all to leave.*

too many times i let myself believe
that i could love the devil
right out of any man,

but that was before i realized
it's a full-time job without
benefits or overtime pay.

—*there are much better careers.*

some days i wake up & think,
i would still do anything
for the person
you made me think
you were.

—it's too bad he doesn't exist.

i've learned that not everyone is worthy
of a redemption arc.

—*make sure they know consequences are real.*

there are days when she wants so badly to
escape her life for something simple & carefree—

to wake up in a cramped cottage
with a tangled & overgrown garden
where she can get drunk on tea
among butterflies & faeries.

oh, what a dream that would be.
she would never have to see anyone again.

—*magic still has to exist somewhere, right?*

as much as i sometimes feel like breaking,
i have never been *broken*.

if i have survived every bad thing
that's ever happened to me,
then doesn't that mean that
i will keep on surviving them?

—*never shall i fall from my throne.*

they say you should always try
to ask flowers for permission
before you go & pluck them
from the ground.

they may not breathe as we do,
but they still deserve respect,
don't they?

well, i am not a flower.
i am a human being.

asking permission
is not a choice.

—*you won't touch me again in this lifetime or any other.*

you'll regret ever raising a hand to me
with the intention of doing
anything other than gently
tucking my hair behind my ear
or wiping an eyelash from my cheek.

—*so mote it be.*

if being in love with you was
as cold & hopeless as eternal winter,

then learning to love myself was
as warm & relieving as
stepping out into a spring day
after a year locked indoors.

—*i am determined to heal.*

if you're with me,
you'll always have competition,

for i am without a doubt
my greatest, fiercest,
& most essential love.

in conclusion,
i will always come first.

—*hopelessly devoted to myself.*

when my heart shatters again,
i know i can always count
on my mother to show me
how to repair it.

bless her wisdom.
bless her selflessness.
bless her compassion.
bless her gentleness.

bless her *everything*.

may i grow to be
even half the woman she is.

—*she's the blueprint.*

bless my mother's anger.

i know if anyone should ever
try to inflict pain upon me,
she'll bring the whole earth
to its knees to get justice for it.

—*i wouldn't mess with her wrath.*

can i overcome the worst things
that have ever happened to me?

can i heal from the harshest words
that have ever been said to me?

can i keep going, knowing
how the world treats girls like me?

—*am i resilient enough?*

"oh yes, my darling,
you are certainly resilient enough.

you have no idea
how many people you inspire

just by having the courage
to face another morning."

—*they will undoubtedly write poems
in your honor one day.*

in a hushed voice, she says to me,

"when they drag you through hell,
do not simply accept it.

do not just give in.

go on & reign over the very flames
that were meant to be your end.

wear them as a crown."

—*show them who's queen.*

acknowledgments

i. *my spouse, parker lee*—thank you for making sure i never run out of pumpkin spice lattes.

ii. *christine day & mira kennedy*—thank you for always being the first eyes on my work & for helping me make it the best it can possibly be!

iii. *janaina medeiros*—thank you for always so beautifully bringing my ideas to life with your illustrations!

iv. *my family*—thank you for always having my back & for never doubting my abilities.

v. *my readers*—thank you for reading my words, whether this is your first book or your eighth!

about the author

amanda lovelace (she/they) is the author of several bestselling poetry titles, including her celebrated "women are some kind of magic" series as well as her new "you are your own fairy tale" trilogy. she is also the co-creator of the *believe in your own magic oracle deck*. when she isn't reading, writing, or drinking a much-needed cup of coffee, you can find her casting spells from her home in a (very) small town on the jersey shore, where she resides with her poet-spouse & their three cats.

index

Ssswish!

Flying Tree Snakes

Look up in the trees!
This flying tree snake
glides from branch
to branch.

body

branch

Sleeping Snakes

See the sleepy snakes curl up in coils.

coil

Ssssh!

Can you slither
and hiss like a snake?

Glossary

Camouflage
[KAM-uh-flahj]
A way for animals to disguise their appearance to blend in with their surroundings

Egg
A soft, leathery shell with a baby snake growing inside

Fang
A large, hollow tooth that shoots out venom

Jaws
Bones that open and close the mouth

Pit Organs
Special sensors found in pits between their eyes and noses that allow pit vipers to sense heat from their prey

Scales
Small, smooth plates that cover the skin

Tongue
A mouth part that can smell, touch, and taste

Venom
A deadly chemical that some snakes inject into their prey by biting them

Index

Quiz

Answer the questions to see what you have learned. Check your answers in the key below.

Which snake am I?

1. I can open my jaws wide, and I eat lizards and frogs.

2. I bite with sharp fangs, and I have pit organs on my face.

3. I rattle my tail when I am angry.

4. I can hide in leaves using camouflage.

5. I can glide through the air from one tree branch to another.

1. A parrot snake 2. A pit viper 3. A rattlesnake
4. A Gaboon viper 5. A flying tree snake